EXPLORING THE STATES

Wisconsin

THE BADGER STATE

by Amy Rechner

ROCKFORD PUBLIC LIBRARY

BELLWETHER MEDIA • MINNEAPOLIS, MN

Note to Librarians, Teachers, and Parents:

Blastoff! Readers are carefully developed by literacy experts and combine standards-based content with developmentally appropriate text.

Level 1 provides the most support through repetition of high-frequency words, light text, predictable sentence patterns, and strong visual support.

Level 2 offers early readers a bit more challenge through varied simple sentences, increased text load, and less repetition of high-frequency words.

Level 3 advances early-fluent readers toward fluency through increased text and concept load, less reliance on visuals, longer sentences, and more literary language.

Level 4 builds reading stamina by providing more text per page, increased use of punctuation, greater variation in sentence patterns, and increasingly challenging vocabulary.

Level 5 encourages children to move from "learning to read" to "reading to learn" by providing even more text, varied writing styles, and less familiar topics.

Whichever book is right for your reader, Blastoff! Readers are the perfect books to build confidence and encourage a love of reading that will last a lifetime!

This edition first published in 2014 by Bellwether Media, Inc.

No part of this publication may be reproduced in whole or in part without written permission of the publisher. For information regarding permission, write to Bellwether Media, Inc., Attention: Permissions Department, 5357 Penn Avenue South, Minneapolis, MN 55419.

Library of Congress Cataloging-in-Publication Data
Rechner, Amy.
Wisconsin / by Amy Rechner.
pages cm. – (Blastoff! readers. Exploring the states)
Includes bibliographical references and index.
Summary: "Developed by literacy experts for students in grades three through seven, this book introduces young readers to the geography and culture of Wisconsin"– Provided by publisher.
ISBN 978-1-62617-050-6 (hardcover : alk. paper)
1. Wisconsin–Juvenile literature. I. Title.
F581.3.R43 2013
977.5–dc23
2013002423

Printed in the United States of America, North Mankato, MN.

Table of Contents

Where Is Wisconsin?

Wisconsin sits in the middle of the **Great Lakes** region of the **Midwest**. Minnesota and Iowa are its neighbors to the west. The Mississippi River forms part of the western border. To the north lie Lake Superior and Michigan's Upper **Peninsula**. Lake Michigan borders the state to the east. To the south is Illinois.

Most of Wisconsin's population lives in the southern part of the state. Madison, the state capital, is in the south. The major cities of Milwaukee, Racine, and Kenosha cluster in the southeastern corner.

Minnesota

fun fact

Wisconsin is nicknamed the Badger State. In the 1800s, miners in the state were called badgers because they lived in carved-out caves like badger dens.

Lake Superior

Michigan

Wisconsin

Green Bay

Mississippi River

Wisconsin Dells

Lake Michigan

Milwaukee

★

Racine

Madison

Kenosha

Iowa

Illinois

5

History

Native American tribes shared Wisconsin's forests, lakes, and streams for about 12,000 years. In 1634, French explorer Jean Nicolet arrived from Canada. French traders and **missionaries** soon followed. In 1763, the British gained control of Wisconsin. They lost it to the United States after the **Revolutionary War**. Wisconsin became a state in 1848.

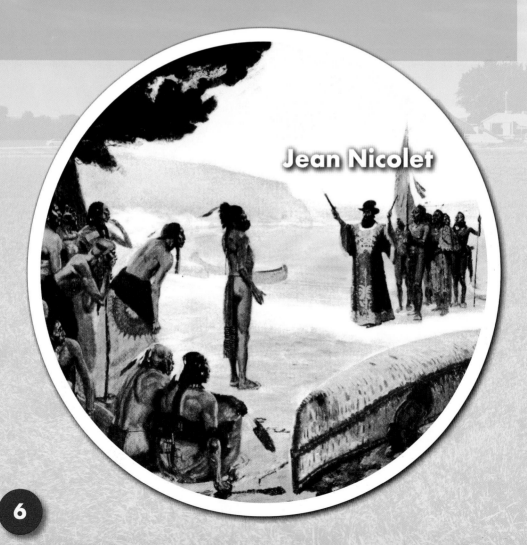

Jean Nicolet

Wisconsin Timeline!

1634: French explorer Jean Nicolet lands near what is now Green Bay.

1763: England wins the French and Indian War. The British take land that includes Wisconsin from the French.

1783: The British lose Wisconsin when the American colonies win the Revolutionary War.

1848: Wisconsin becomes the thirtieth state.

1884: The Ringling Brothers give their first circus performance in Baraboo.

1919: Wisconsin is the first state to approve the Nineteenth Amendment, which gives women the right to vote.

1967: The Green Bay Packers win the first Super Bowl. They go on to win the second Super Bowl in 1968.

2008: Heavy rainfall causes Lake Delton in the Wisconsin Dells to overflow its banks. The lake empties completely and destroys surrounding homes.

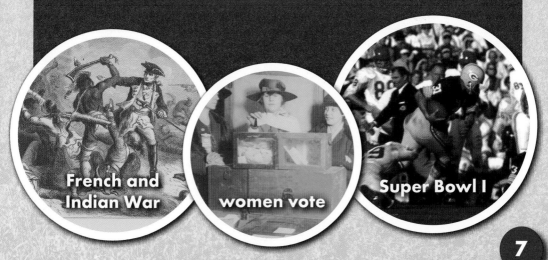

French and Indian War

women vote

Super Bowl I

The Land

Did you know?
Wisconsin has more than 15,000 lakes, but less than half of them have names.

The **glaciers** that once covered the northern United States created Wisconsin's beautiful landscape. Forests spread across the northern half of the state. Southern Wisconsin has rich farmland. To the east, the Kettle **Moraine** region holds miles of hills and small lakes that were formed by the glaciers.

Wisconsin has thousands of natural lakes. The largest is Lake Winnebago in the east. The Wisconsin River runs down the center of the state. Wisconsin has cold, snowy winters and hot summers. Winds blowing from Lakes Michigan and Superior keep waterside communities cool. In winter, snowfall is greater along the shore.

The Wisconsin Dells

The Wisconsin **Dells** were created
thousands of years ago by water from
a melting glacier. A deep, narrow
gorge was carved out of the land.
Now the Wisconsin River flows through
it. Towering sandstone and rock
formations line the river. Stand Rock
is the most famous formation. This tall,
mushroom-shaped rock stands next to
the river **bluffs**.

The Wisconsin Dells have been a
popular vacation spot since the 1800s.
Visitors can explore the natural rock
formations on foot or in touring vehicles
called Wisconsin Ducks.
The Ducks can drive
on land and float
in water.

Wisconsin Duck

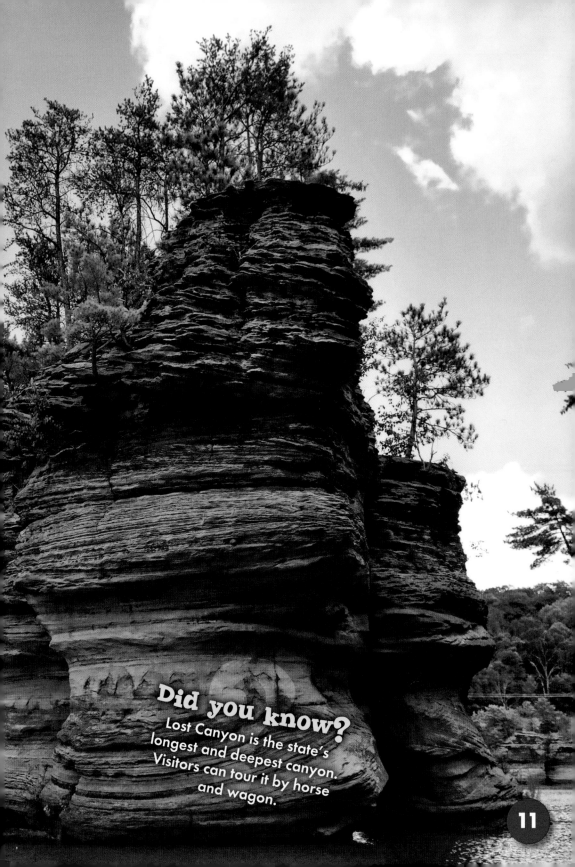

Did you know?
Lost Canyon is the state's longest and deepest canyon. Visitors can tour it by horse and wagon.

Wildlife

Wisconsin's dense forests provide shelter for many woodland animals. Deer, black bears, and porcupines live in the northern woods and central hills. Foxes and raccoons are common throughout the state. The gray wolf, a protected animal, has returned to Wisconsin.

Cardinals and red-winged blackbirds fill the woods with birdsong. Ferns and wildflowers thrive beneath the shade of trees. Lakes and rivers hold perch, walleye, and bass.

porcupine

red-winged blackbird

fun fact

Wisconsin's state fish is a muskellunge, or muskie. The largest muskie ever caught in the state weighed nearly 70 pounds (32 kilograms) and was more than 5 feet (1.5 meters) long.

muskellunge

gray wolf

Landmarks

Did you know?
The Apostle Islands National Lakeshore is on Lake Superior. Boats from the town of Bayfield take hikers, fishers, and campers to explore the untamed islands.

Wisconsin has many unusual places to see. The House on the Rock is a maze of unique items in Spring Green. The house holds suits of armor, model ships, musical instruments, and much more. Nearby is the Cave of the Mounds. Tours of the cave show delicate rock formations that are up to one million years old.

House on
the Rock

Circus World

The small town of Mount Horeb is called the Troll Capital of the World. More than fifteen carved wooden trolls line the town's Main Street, called the Trollway. In Baraboo, Circus World features year-round circus displays and magic shows. Summer brings daily circus performances under the Big Top.

Milwaukee

Milwaukee's position as a **port** on Lake Michigan helped to make it the state's largest city. Settlers came from Europe and the eastern United States by boat or train. Thousands of German **immigrants** created a community that kept their **traditions** alive. Irish, African Americans, and many other groups also lend their traditions to Milwaukee's **diverse** culture.

Milwaukee's parks and beaches draw crowds in the summer. The Discovery World Museum on the lakefront explores science, technology, and the environment. The indoor gardens of Mitchell Park Conservatory offer year-round warmth.

Mitchell Park Conservatory

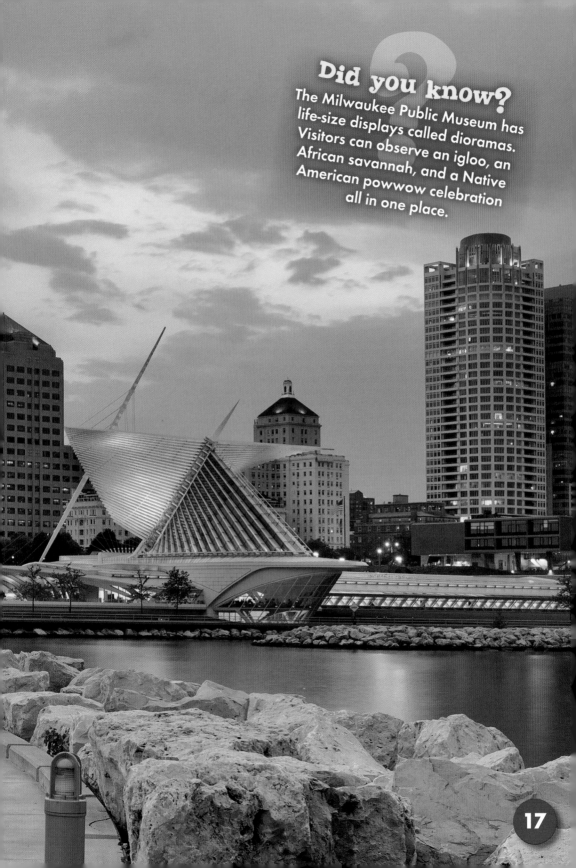

Did you know?

The Milwaukee Public Museum has life-size displays called dioramas. Visitors can observe an igloo, an African savannah, and a Native American powwow celebration all in one place.

fun fact !

The city of Kohler is the location of one of the world's most famous toilet manufacturers. It is about one hour away from Green Bay, the Toilet Paper Capital of the World.

Cows are part of the scenery in Wisconsin's countryside. The state is called America's Dairyland. It has more dairy farms than any other state. Farmers produce milk for cheese, butter, ice cream, and other dairy products. Other farmers grow crops of corn, cranberries, and **ginseng**.

Wisconsin factories hire workers to build machinery, motorcycles, and electronics. Paper, cleaning supplies, and food products are also made in the state. Many Wisconsinites have **service jobs** in banks, hotels, and restaurants. **Tourists** keep them especially busy during the summer months.

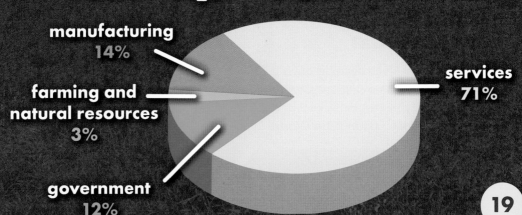

Where People Work in Wisconsin

manufacturing
14%

farming and natural resources
3%

government
12%

services
71%

Playing

Wisconsin is an outdoor playground in all seasons. The thousands of lakes and rivers are full of fish for catching. Boating and waterskiing are also popular. Cross-country skiers and snowmobilers head out when the temperatures drop. In summer, the northern forests attract campers and hikers. Hunters take to the woods in fall.

Wisconsinites enjoy the same places tourists do. Door County and the Dells are popular vacation spots. Outdoor concerts and theater performances draw crowds in the summer. Wisconsin has several professional and college sports teams. Football fans root for the Green Bay Packers and the University of Wisconsin Badgers.

fun fact

The Wisconsin Dells became an attraction because of their natural beauty. Today the region is known as the Water Park Capital of the World.

Danish Kringle

Ingredients:

1 box refrigerated piecrusts, softened as directed on box

2/3 cup chopped pecans

1/3 cup packed brown sugar

3 tablespoons butter, softened

White icing

Water

Directions:

1. Heat oven to 375°F. Place uncovered piecrust flat on ungreased large cookie sheet.

2. In medium bowl, mix pecans, brown sugar, and butter. Sprinkle over half of piecrust to within 3/4 inch of edge.

3. Brush edge with water. Fold piecrust over filling. Move kringle to center of cookie sheet. Press edge with fork to seal. Then poke top with fork.

4. Bake 17 to 22 minutes or until golden brown. Cool 5 minutes. Drizzle white icing on top.

Cornish pasty

cheese curds

Familiar foods in Wisconsin reflect the state's heritage. People go to Milwaukee for the best German food, especially bratwursts. In Racine, pastries called Kringles come from the area's Danish settlers. The small town of Mineral Point is known for its Cornish pasties. These large pastries are filled with meat and vegetables. Early miners ate pasties for lunch.

Cheese and frozen custard are sold at small stands throughout Wisconsin. Another state tradition is the Friday night fish fry. Fresh fish and french fries are served every week.

Festivals

Summerfest

Did you know?
The nation's largest Native American festival is held in Milwaukee. Members of Wisconsin's eleven tribes invite other Native Americans to join them in a powwow.

Wisconsin loves festivals. Milwaukee's Summerfest is considered the world's largest music festival. Up to a million fans come each year to see performances by more than 800 bands. The Summerfest grounds are also used for weekend events that celebrate the city's diverse groups. German Fest, Polish Fest, and Irish Fest draw Wisconsinites from across the state.

Hayward hosts the Lumberjack World Championships in July. Men and women compete in sawing, chopping, pole climbing, and logrolling. AirVenture brings action to the skies over Oshkosh each year. Visitors get up close to military planes, early **biplanes**, and even homemade planes. Daredevil pilots perform stunts overhead in daylight and dark.

fun fact

Lake Geneva hosts the U.S. National Snow Sculpting Competition during its Winterfest celebration. Teams carve detailed sculptures from 9-foot (3-meter) blocks of snow.

The Green Bay Packers

The Green Bay Packers are one of the NFL's most successful teams. They have won more world championships than any other team in the league. The Green Bay Packers are also the only professional team owned by the public. Any fan can buy a piece of the Pack!

People from other states liked to make fun of Packers fans. They called them "cheeseheads" because of Wisconsin's dairy farms. Wisconsinites didn't let the name-calling get to them. Instead, they started wearing hats shaped like giant wedges of cheese. Packers fans still support their state by wearing their cheeseheads with true Wisconsin pride!

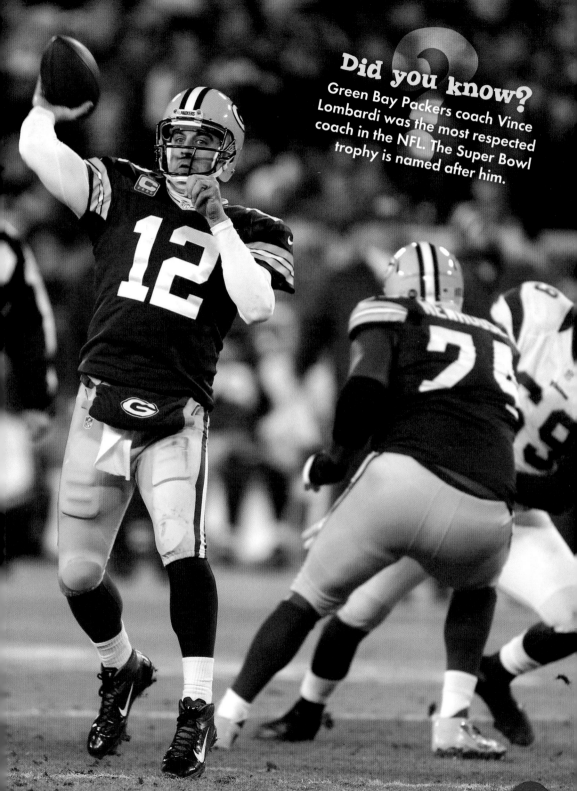

27

WISCONSIN

FORWARD

1848

Wisconsin's Flag

The Wisconsin flag is blue with "Wisconsin" and "1848" spelled out in white. In the center of the flag is the state's coat of arms. A ribbon reading "Forward" flies above it.

State Flower
wood violet

State Nicknames:	The Badger State America's Dairyland
State Motto:	"Forward"
Year of Statehood:	1848
Capital City:	Madison
Other Major Cities:	Milwaukee, Green Bay, Kenosha, Racine
Population:	5,686,986 (2010)
Area:	65,496 square miles (169,634 square kilometers); Wisconsin is the 23rd largest state.
Major Industries:	dairy, paper, machinery, tourism
Natural Resources:	farmland, forests, freshwater, copper, iron, lead, zinc
State Government:	99 representatives; 33 senators
Federal Government:	8 representatives; 2 senators
Electoral Votes:	10

State Animal
badger

State Bird
American robin

Glossary

biplanes—planes with two sets of wings, one placed above the other

bluffs—high, steep banks or cliffs

dells—wooded valleys

diverse—made up of many different types or coming from many different backgrounds

ginseng—an herb used for health benefits; ginseng is grown in Asia and North America.

glaciers—massive sheets of ice that cover large areas of land

gorge—a deep, narrow valley with steep, rocky sides

Great Lakes—five large freshwater lakes on the border between the United States and Canada

immigrants—people who leave one country to live in another country

Midwest—a region made up of 12 states in the north-central United States

missionaries—people who travel to spread a religious faith

moraine—a pile of earth and stones left by a glacier

native—originally from a specific place

peninsula—a section of land that extends out from a larger piece of land and is almost completely surrounded by water

port—a harbor where ships can dock

Revolutionary War—the war between 1775 and 1783 in which the United States fought for independence from Great Britain

service jobs—jobs that perform tasks for people or businesses

tourists—people who travel to visit another place

traditions—customs, ideas, or beliefs handed down from one generation to the next

To Learn More

AT THE LIBRARY
Dornfeld, Margaret, and Richard Hantula. *Wisconsin*. New York, N.Y.: Marshall Cavendish Benchmark, 2011.

Reischel, Rob. *Green Bay Packers*. Edina, Minn.: ABDO Pub. Co., 2011.

Wilder, Laura Ingalls. *Little House in the Big Woods*. New York, N.Y.: Harper & Brothers, 1932.

ON THE WEB
Learning more about Wisconsin is as easy as 1, 2, 3.

1. Go to www.factsurfer.com.

2. Enter "Wisconsin" into the search box.

3. Click the "Surf" button and you will see a list of related Web sites.

With factsurfer.com, finding more information is just a click away.

Index